OUR CELTIC HE

CW00336333

SAINT ANDREW PRESS

OUR CELTIC HERITAGE

*Looking at Our Own Faith
in the Light of Celtic Christianity*

A STUDY GUIDE
FOR CHRISTIAN GROUPS

CHRIS KING

First published in 1997 by
SAINT ANDREW PRESS
121 George Street, Edinburgh EH2 4YN

Copyright © Chris King 1997

ISBN 0 7152 0729 6

All rights reserved. No part of this publication may be reproduced or transmitted in any form or by any means, electronic or mechanical, including photocopy, recording, or information storage and retrieval system, without permission in writing from the publisher. This book is sold, subject to the condition that it shall not, by way of trade or otherwise, be lent, re-sold, hired out or otherwise circulated without the publisher's prior consent.

British Library Cataloguing in Publication Data
A catalogue record for this book
is available from the British Library.

ISBN 0715207296

Cover design by Mark Blackadder.
Cover and internal photographs by Paul Turner.
Internal line drawings by Sheila Cant.
Typesetting by Lesley A Taylor.
Printed and **bound** by Athenaeum Press Ltd, Gateshead, Tyne & Wear.

Our Celtic Heritage

Introduction   1
   Summary Outline   4
   Some of the Challenges of Celtic Christianity   6
   Chronology   7
   Notes for the Leader   8
   General Resource Sheet – *Celtic Prayers*   11

Session 1   **The Caim and the High Cross**   17
                 Resource Sheet 1   30
Session 2   **God the Creator**   37
                 Resource Sheet 2   46
Session 3   **Never too busy to pray**   53
                 Resource Sheet 3   66
Session 4   **The Trinity**   75
                 Resource Sheet 4   84
Session 5   **'St Patrick's Breastplate'**   93
                 Resource Sheet 5   111

Music Sheet 1   'All God's Creatures got a Place ... '   115
Music Sheet 2   'May the Road rise with You'   117
Resources   118
References   119
Acknowledgements   120

CONTENTS

To my husband, ALAN
without whose unfailing support and encouragement
this book would never have been written

DEDICATION

This book has grown from a number of Celtic retreats.
Thanks are due to all who took part in them.

A friend came to one of these retreats
feeling that Celtic spirituality had little to offer him,
but he found himself writing the beautiful prayer below.

This book is offered in the hope that many, like him,
may be enriched by discovering more
about our Celtic Christians and their prayers.

God in my breathing, help me to see
    The air which contains Thee.
God in my speaking, help me to know
    Thy Word become enfleshed below.
God in my praying, teach me how
    To know you, love you, serve you now.

OUR CELTIC HERITAGE

Our Celtic Heritage is a study guide for Christian groups wishing to explore some of the insights of Celtic Spirituality. It challenges us to look afresh at our own relationships to God, to each other, and to God's world. Each Session looks at one or more aspect and encourages discussion of its relevance to, and impact upon, our daily lives.

Each Session contains background information, discussion topics, reflections and suggestions for times of prayer. Celtic prayers, both ancient and modern, are provided on Resource pages. Although each Session will contain input from the leader, the emphasis is on group exploration and discovery, with time for prayer and reflection.

SUMMARY OUTLINE

Session 1

THE CAIM AND THE HIGH CROSS

1	Introduction	*page* 19
2	Celts from 800 BC to the Time of Christ	19
3	The Caim	21
4	The High Cross	24
5	The Celts and Outreach	26
6	Group Prayer	28

Session 2

GOD THE CREATOR

1	Recap	*page* 39
2	The Celtic View of God	39
3	God the Creator	40
4	Group Prayer	45

Session 3

NEVER TOO BUSY TO PRAY

1	Recap	*page* 55
2	Never too busy to pray	55
3	Writing Celtic Prayers	56
4	Group Prayer	57
5	A Celtic Dance	58
6	Celtic Art	59

Session 4

THE TRINITY

1	Recap	*page* 77
2	The Trinity	77
3	Symbols for the Holy Spirit	79
4	Prayers of Protection	80
5	Scripture Prayers	81
6	Group Prayer	83

Session 5

'ST PATRICK'S BREASTPLATE'

1	Preparation for Service	*page* 95
2	Introduction to 'St Patrick's Breastplate'	95
3	Reflection on Verses I–IV	97
4	Reflection on Verses V–VIIa	101
5	Meditation on Verse 7b	103
6	Conclusion to 'St Patrick's Breastplate'	106
7	Reflective Discussion on the Series	106
8	'Open hand' Meditation	107
9	Short Celtic-style Service	108

SOME OF THE CHALLENGES
OF CELTIC CHRISTIANITY

Celtic Christianity can challenge us in a number of ways. Although these challenges are brought out during the various Sessions in this book, it may be helpful to be aware of some of them beforehand.

1   Since Celtic Christianity predates many of our traditional views and customs, we may be challenged to consider which of our traditions are essential to our faith. This can be particularly helpful when assessing why some people are put off by 'the Church'.

2   The Celts had a great desire to evangelise and did so by building upon whatever faith people already had, without destroying or suppressing the good in the cultures they encountered. This may challenge us to look afresh at both local and international evangelism.

3   Celts had a deep love and concern for nature as part of God's world. This may challenge today's exploitational approach to the natural world.

4   The Celts preached a victorious message. Often modern Christianity is concerned to be popular and inoffensive. We may be challenged to consider the message offered by Christianity today.

5   Celts believed in a spirit world around us, and in the unity of the spiritual and the material. We may be challenged to look at:
    (a)   the materialistic attitudes of the modern world;
    (b)   the frequent acceptance that there is a scientific explanation for all things.

6 Celtic religion permeated the whole of life. Today we often emphasise the special acts of worship in special places and this can have the unfortunate effect of divorcing our religion from our daily life. We can be challenged to consider the 'Sunday Christian' approach to faith.

7 The Celtic Church disagreed strongly with Augustine's theory of original sin. Much of our understanding of Christianity has been influenced by theologians throughout the centuries. We can be challenged to see if we feel their interpretations of the Bible are valid for us today.

These are some of the ways in which the group may be challenged. It is unlikely that *all* of these issues will emerge during the following Sessions, but you may wish to initiate related discussions at additional times.

CHRONOLOGY

AD 313*	Edict of Milan – Christianity tolerated in Roman Empire.
325	Council of Nicaea – first general Council of the Church.
354–430	St Augustine of Hippo. He argued for idea of original sin and led attack on Pelagius.
360–430	Pelagius – Celtic British theologian condemned as a heretic in 418.
389–461	Saint Patrick.
397	Whithorn founded by St Ninian.
410	Last Roman legions withdrawn from Britain.
410	Sack of Rome by Alaric the Goth.
432	Patrick went to Ireland.
455	Rome pillaged by Vandals.
480–550	Saint Benedict.

515	Battle of Mount Badon – West Saxon advance halted by Britons, possibly led by Arthur.
521–597	St Columba.
540–615	St Columbanus.
–612	St Kentigern or Mungo.
565	Iona founded by St Columba.
570–632	Mohammed.
590	Gregory the Great becomes Pope.
597	St Augustine arrives in Kent, sent by the Pope to bring the Church in Britain under Roman authority.
600–750	Irish monks were most important religious influence in France and then through much of Western Europe.
–651	St Aidan.
634	Lindisfarne founded by St Aidan.
638	Jerusalem captured by Moslems.
664	Synod of Whitby.
8th–9th centuries	*Lindisfarne Gospels* and *The Book of Kells*

[*many of these dates may only be approximate]

NOTES FOR THE LEADER

Timing

There are five Sessions, each expected to last 90 minutes. If you wish to include time for coffee, please extend the Session accordingly.

The material allows for a longer period of time for discussion and a shorter period for prayer. You may wish to alter the balance. In this case you could either reduce the number of discussion topics, or allow more time for each Session. All timings are advisory only. Feel free to alter them as appropriate.

- You will need a Bible for Sessions 1, 2 and 4.

- You will need a tape of quiet background music for Sessions 2, 3 and 4. This should have no words and should not include well known tunes.

There are boxes headed 'Read aloud ...'. Invite different members of the group to read these aloud.

Session 1

- Take time at the beginning of the Session for members of the group to introduce themselves and for you to outline how the evenings will proceed.

Session 2

- If possible ask one of the group to learn the song 'All God's Creatures got a Place ...' (see pages 115-116), so that they could lead it for 'God made the World and he was pleased with it' [see section 3(a) on page 40].

- You will need a plant or flower arrangement, or a picture of nature depicting, for example, flowers, mountains, the sea shore or wood-lands, for the time of reflection entitled 'God is creating now'. You will also need an audio tape recording or a copy of the words of the Hymn 'Oh Lord my God, when I in awesome wonder' (*Songs of God's People,* Hymn no. 86) [see section 3(b) on page 43].

Session 3

- You will need paper and pens for each member of the group for the section entitled 'Writing Celtic Prayers' [see section 3, page 56].

- For the 'Celtic Dance' in section 5 (page 58) you will need sufficient space for the group to stand in a circle and to move slowly round. You will also need to familiarise yourself with the dance beforehand. Although some people might be reluctant to join in the dance, it is worthwhile to encourage everyone to participate. Since it is a slow, walking dance, most people will in the end enjoy it. If possible, find someone who can play the tune or lead the singing for the group. The music is on page 117.

Session 4

- You will need paper, pens and a Bible for each member of the group for the Reflection in section 5 (see page 82).

Session 5

- Hopefully members of the group will bring various items for the service at the end of this Session (see page 108). You will need to made yourself aware of the type of contribution (hymn, prayer, *etc*) and decide on the order to incorporate them.

- During the service you will need to invite people to make their contribution at the appropriate time.

GENERAL RESOURCE SHEET

CELTIC PRAYERS

The chanting of the birds I hear – good to draw man's tears:
Each of them answers the other. Does not the whole church do so?

~ A World made Whole ~

God's will would I do,
My own will bridle;

God's due would I give,
My own due yield;

God's path would I travel,
My own path refuse;

Christ's death would I ponder.
My own death remember;

God's judgement would I judge,
My own judgement guard;

Christ's redemption would I seize,
My own ransom work,

The love of Christ would I feel,
My own love know.

~ Carmina Gadelica ~

There is a mother's heart in the heart of God.

~ Traditional Celtic Saying ~

May mercy be my lip's attire,
May kindness to my face be lent,
May chasteness be on my desire,
And wisdom be in mine intent.

~ Praying with Highland Christians ~

You are risen,
Let trumpets proclaim.
You are risen,
Let sun brightly flame.
You are risen,
Dark night is past.
You are risen,
Hope will now last.
You are risen,
Let us not dread.
You are risen,
Back from the dead.
You are risen,
Lord of the skies.
You are risen,
Help is to arise.

~ Tides and Seasons ~

Thou commandest peace
Thou gavest peace
Thou didst leave peace.
Give us, O Lord
Thy peace from heaven
and make this day peaceful,
And the remaining days of our life
Do Thou dispose in Thy peace.
Through our Lord.

~ Stowe Missal ~

If anybody enters the path of repentance
it is sufficient to advance a step every day.
Do not wish to be a charioteer.

~ Rule of Comgall ~

Weakly I go from the load within
Deeply repenting with woe my sin.
I acknowledge the faith of my God this day
With love from my heart and hope always.
From the foot of thy cross I came to Thee
O Jesus Lord, bow down to me.

~ Religious Songs ~

Good shepherd
> be over me to shelter me
> under me to uphold me
> behind me to direct me
> before me to lead me
> about me to protect me
> ever with me to save me
> above me to lift me
and bring me to the green pasture

~ Edge of Glory ~

O Father, O Son. O Holy Spirit,
Forgive me [us] my sins,
O only-begotten Son of the heavenly Father
Forgive.
O one God, O true God, O chief God,
O God of one substance, O God only mighty,
in three Persons, truly pitiful,
Forgive.

~ St Cieran ~

God, bless the world and all that is therein,
God, bless my spouse and my children,
God, bless the eye that is in my head,
And bless, O God, the handling of my hand;

What time I rise in morning early,
What time I lie down late in bed,
    Bless my rising in the morning early,
    And my lying down late in bed.

~ Carmina Gadelica ~

I am giving Thee worship with my whole life,
    I am giving Thee assent with my whole power,
I am giving Thee praise with my whole tongue,
    I am giving Thee honour with my whole utterance.

I am giving Thee love with my whole devotion,
    I am giving Thee kneeling with my whole desire,
I am giving Thee love with my whole heart,
    I am giving Thee affection with my whole sense;
I am giving Thee my existence with my whole mind,
    I am giving Thee my soul, O God of all the gods.

~ Carmina Gadelica ~

The blessing of God be upon you, that good come to you;
The blessing of Christ be upon you, that good be done to you;
The blessing of the Holy Ghost be yours,
    that good be the course of your life,
    each day of your rising, each night of your lying down,
    for evermore, Amen.

~ God in Our Midst ~

THE CAIM
AND THE
HIGH CROSS

1   Introduction   (5 mins)

During these five Sessions we hope to explore various aspects of Celtic spirituality and discover what it has to say to us today. We will consider how the Celts saw God, how they saw themselves and others, and how they saw their environment. We will also study in more detail the great prayer of St Patrick. In no way was the Celtic society ideal. Many things that happened we would find unacceptable today. Nevertheless much that is of lasting value can arise out of what is, in the best sense, primitive – and we may all learn from the insights of the Celts.

The hope is to approach the Sessions by offering enough information on a particular topic to enable us to explore it either in group discussions, or in private prayer, or in writing our own Celtic-style prayers. This is very much a group approach to seeing how we can gain from looking at Celtic spirituality.

2   Celts from 800 BC to the Time of Christ   (10 mins)

Individually

- Read quickly through the General Resource Sheet on pages 11-15. [There will be more time later in this Session to return to these prayers.]

The Celts were a large number of tribes, bound together more by blood-ties and customs than by land. From about eighth century BC they lived on the high lands across Spain, Germany, France and Switzerland and were as important a civilisation as the Greeks or the Romans. They were largely cattle and horse breeders who became wealthy through trading, particularly those tribes who controlled the main river routes of the Rhine, Rhone and Seine. They were a fierce people who enjoyed fighting, but also storytelling and poetry. They lived in clans, each ruled by its own king.

As far as history is concerned, they had two great weaknesses – they did not like writing and they were too independent to acknowledge one over-king. The first of these meant that the only written records of the Celts, apart from trading papers, were written by their conquerors. Therefore, until archaeological evidence was discovered, historians were unaware how important a civilisation the Celts were. Their second weakness meant that they were gradually defeated by organised armies like the Romans. Nevertheless, before this happened they managed to sack Rome in 390 BC, and by 279 BC they had taken over most of Europe. A large part became known as Gaul, a name by which some Celtic tribes were known. One province of Asia Minor was known by the slight variation of 'Galatia' – the Galatians were in fact Celts.

Some centuries before the time of Christ, these tribes began to move across Europe to escape from more dominant tribes and to gain more land as their population grew. By the time of Christ, most of the Celts had been forced to flee to the edges of Europe – to Gaul in France, to Britain and to Ireland. The great Celtic civilisation was nearing its end. However, many of these Celts became converted to Christianity and, during the Dark Ages, it was largely the Irish Celts who kept Christianity alive and eventually emerged as missionaries to take the Gospel throughout Europe.

3 The Caim (25 mins)

The Celts were very conscious that God was all around them. They would help themselves to be more aware of this by drawing a circle around themselves, usually with their arm outstretched, and physically sweep out a circle. They would then concentrate on God's love, peace and joy filling that circle: filling themselves and the area around them. They gave themselves to God and were filled by him. This is the Caim.

The Caim is not magic. It is an aid to make us more aware of the reality of God's presence and it helps to re-tune us to this reality.

David Adam likens this to radio or television waves. They are always around us, but we are unaware of them until we switch the set on. In the same way we often forget that God is here. The Caim is a way of switching on and tuning in. We need to focus on the fact that we are because God is – we need to remember his power and presence and try not to live our lives in our own strength.

Individually

- Read silently through the prayers on pages 30-32 [see Resource Sheet 1].

Read aloud

- 2 Corinthians 4: 7-9.
  [NOTE: Supreme power is God's, not ours:
  We are often troubled, but not crushed;
  in doubt, but never despair;
  have many enemies,
  but are never without a friend.]

Read aloud

- The Caim Prayer, 'Circle me Lord', on page 31.

Written prayers obviously need words. However, when we use the Caim we do not have to say a prayer – we can simply be with God, bringing ourselves and others before him. The Celts might have extended the circle mentally to include their family, village, or anyone else they wished to be surrounded by God that day. This is a lovely way of praying for ourselves, our family, workplace, friends, or even enemies.

There is a poem that speaks of this:

He drew a ring which shut me out,
Heretic, rebel, a thing to flout.
But love and I had wit to win,
We drew a circle that took him in.

Here is a Caim prayer which can be adapted for all occasions:

> *Lord, circle this room /office /town /traffic jam*
> *Fill it with your presence.*
> *Your presence is peace /love /joy.*

['Use a different appropriate attribute for as many verses as you like.]

Praying the Caim

Individually

- Take 5 mins to pray the Caim how you like: physically drawing the circle round yourself if you wish; otherwise doing it mentally. You may wish to find your own space in which to be quiet. Use a prayer from the sheet, or just concentrate on God's presence. Start by praying it for yourself. Then try praying it for others.

Discuss
(in small groups of four or five)

- For which of the following would you feel happy using the Caim in your prayer life – to start the day at work; praying for the sick; praying for those you do not get on with.

- Can you think of any other occasions when you might use the Caim?

4   The High Cross   (20 mins)

The cross with all arms of equal length is an extremely old symbol representing the four directions – North, South, East and West – and as such is used by many spiritualities. Pagan Celts might well have been familiar with such a cross. Christian Celts would try to build on familiar symbols. They used the Christian cross with a circle joining the arms, possibly retaining a symbol familiar to sun-worshippers, but giving it the Christian interpretation of the crown of victory won for us by Christ. It also echoes the circle of the Caim, with Christ, as it were, drawing us into his circle of victory. The circle is a symbol of wholeness and completeness – and this too is a prominent theme of Celtic Christianity.

(a)   *The Cross and Victory*

The Celtic crosses were extremely large, standing high up and out in the open air. They proclaimed the victory of Christ. They were used as preaching crosses and also as the focal point for open air services since the churches were often too small for the congregation to gather inside.

(b)   *The Cross and Salvation*

The crucifixion was central to the Celtic faith. It was through Christ's death on the cross that sins could be forgiven. They were very conscious of Christ's suffering.

Turn to the part of the Resource section headed 'The Cross' on page 33. In the mid-eighth century Blathmac wrote a long poem about the life of Jesus.

Read aloud

- The part of Blathmac's poem on page 34.

(c)' *The Cross and Protection*

Celts were very aware of spiritual warfare. Their Christianity was not a promise of an easy life, but a challenge, struggle and battle. They were always conscious of sin, evil and suffering, and of an invisible army waiting to harm them. They believed the cross would protect them. When sudden trouble came on them, they would exclaim 'the Cross of Christ upon us!' as a protection.

'St Patrick's Breastplate' is probably the best known protection prayer. [See page 111.] Many people still cross themselves when they feel threatened.

Individually

- Read the prayer 'Christ's cross over this face … ' from Resource Sheet 1 on page 33.

Discuss
(in groups of four or five)

Celts felt that the human suffering of Christ's death on the cross was central to their faith, since they thereby obtained forgiveness for their sins. They often described the suffering in great detail.

- Do you feel the message of the Churches today places the right amount of emphasis on the physical suffering of Jesus, or should it change? Are representations of Jesus' suffering, such as the Oberammergau plays, helpful?

- The Celtic Church was triumphant and confident in the power of Jesus. What examples of a 'victorious message' can you suggest for our Churches to preach?

5   The Celts and Outreach   (15 mins)

The High Crosses were used as focal points for preaching. The Celtic Church placed great emphasis on going out to others to share the Gospel.

Read aloud

- Acts 17: 22, 23 – Paul at Athens.

The Celtic missionaries grafted their Christian ideas onto the existing pagan culture – hence the blending of the pagan and Christian religions in the prayers. At Rodail, Harris there is a cruciform church of the thirteenth century. The church abuts a much older tower. Around this tower are carvings of birds and beasts, reptiles and fish, and symbols of pagan worship. Here pagan joins with Christian faith.

Columba thought that the best way to defeat paganism was to 'take it over'. Thus he regularly held outdoor services in the middle of the druid's standing stones and 'baptised' these stones by carving crosses on them. About fifty years later an Irish missionary to France, Columbanus, discovered a ruined temple to the goddess Diana at Annegray in the Vosges. He restored it and used it as the church for his new monastery.

Read aloud

- 2 Corinthians 5: 18.

The Celts believed that God was already at work in a place long before the missionaries arrived. It was the missionaries task to discover what God was doing there, to discover to what extent the people worshipped any god, and whether there were already signs of charity and other spiritual fruits. They would then try to build on these. They would acknowledge the worship that was already taking place. If it was pagan, they would challenge it with their own worship. If there was any remnants of earlier Christian worship – there was often a derelict chapel and a so-called priest, even though that might be an hereditary title and the priest knew little about Jesus – they would attempt to use the chapel and teach the priest. Either way, they would try to build on what was already going on. They did not take Christianity to the people so much as reveal the God who was already there.

As the Celtic missionaries came into contact with other established Christian traditions, they found themselves pleading for different traditions to exist side by side, and for a process of assimilation and adaptation rather than confrontation.

Discuss
(in groups of four or five)

The Celtic missionaries tried to find God's presence in the people and the culture they were working with, and then build on this, whilst at the same time denouncing pagan practices.

Does this have anything to say to:

- today's missionary and aid organisations?
- our own outreach in our local communities?

Suggest some ways of outreach which you think the Celts would have liked?

---

6   Group Prayer   (15 mins)

Turn to the Resource Sheet 'Celtic Prayers' on pages 11-15. Spend time looking again at the prayer sheet, noticing the intimacy and simplicity of some of the prayers. [Some Celtic prayers may have seemed very demanding, because the Celts used command statements such as 'The peace of God', where we might say '*May* the peace of God'.]

Invite the group to share a time of prayer, either in silence, sharing Celtic prayers from the sheet, and/or open prayer.

We have looked at:

- reconciliation;
- the victory of the cross;
- outreach and missionary work;
- using the Caim.

The group may wish to use the time of prayer to pray about these.

FOR THE NEXT SESSION

Invite any musicians to bring their instruments to play 'All God's Creatures' (you will find the music score on pages 115-116).

Arrange with the host or hostess for a plant or flower arrangement, or a picture of nature – such as flowers, mountains, sea shore or woodlands – to be available.

RESOURCE SHEET 1

THE CAIM
AND THE HIGH CROSS

THE CAIM

Draw a circle around yourself
Become aware of God filling it with
peace, love, strength

Draw the Caim around your
family,
friends/work place,
church,
village/town,
the hungry …

Circle me Lord

Circle me Lord
Keep protection near
And danger afar

Circle me Lord
Keep hope within
Keep doubt without

Circle me Lord
Keep light near
And darkness afar

Circle me Lord
Keep peace within
Keep evil out.

~ Edge of Glory ~

The compassing of God be upon thee,
    The compassing of the God of life.

The compassing of Christ upon thee
    The compassing of the Christ of love.

The compassing of Spirit be on thee,
    The compassing of the Spirit of grace.

The compassing of the Three be on thee,
    The compassing of the Three preserve thee,
    The compassing of the Three preserve thee.

~ Carmina Gadelica ~

The compassing of God and His right hand
Be upon my form and upon my frame;
The compassing of the High King and the grace of the Trinity
    Be upon me abiding ever eternally,
    Be upon me abiding ever eternally.

May the compassing of the Three shield me in my means,
The compassing of the Three shield me this day,
The compassing of the Three shield me this night
    From hate, from harm, from act, from ill,
    From hate, from harm, from act, from ill.

~ Carmina Gadelica ~

Jesu! Only begotten Son and Lamb of God the Father,
Thou did give the wine-blood of Thy body to buy me from the grave.
    My Christ! My Christ! My shield, my encircler,
    Each day, each night, each light, each dark;
    My Christ! My Christ! My shield, my encircler,
    Each day, each night, each light, each dark;

Be near me, uphold me, my treasure, my triumph,
In my lying, in my standing, in my watching in my sleeping.
    Jesu, Son of Mary! My helper, my encircler.
    Jesu, Son of David! My strength everlasting;
    Jesu, Son of Mary! My helper, my encircler,
    Jesu! Son of David! My strength everlasting.

~ Carmina Gadelica ~

THE CROSS

O Lord who didst suffer Thy tortures for me,
Torn with iron from the head to the knee,
Whose feet and whose hands were nailed to the tree,
Help, Lord! I come seeking protection from Thee.

~ Religious Songs ~

Because the Son of God is being scourged, being punished,
With narrow ropes of hemp to posts of stone,
The spear of venom going through His side,
The crown of thorns going through His head,
Blunt nails going into His feet,
His share of blessed blood being poured
on the stone of the street.

~ from 'Mary's Vision' (Religious Songs) ~

Christ's cross over this face, and thus over my ear.
Christ's cross over this eye,
Christ's cross over this nose.

Christ's cross eastwards facing me,
Christ's cross back towards the sunset.
In the north, in the south,
　　increasingly may Christ's cross straightway be.

Christ's cross up to broad Heaven.
Christ's cross down to earth
Let no evil or hurt come to my body or my soul.

Christ's cross over me as I sit.
Christ's cross over me as I lie.
Christ's cross be all my strength
    until we reach the King of Heaven.

From the top of my head to the mail of my foot,
O Christ, against every danger
    I trust in the protection of the cross.
Till the day of my death, going into this clay,
I shall draw without − Christ's cross over this face.

~ *Threshold of Light* ~

From the Poems of the Son of Blathmac ...

I bitterly lament Christ being crucified ...

Your people seized your son; Mary, they flogged him. There struck him the green reed and fists across ruddy cheeks.

It was a hideous deed that was done to him; that his very mother-kin should crucify the man who had come to save them.
Hands were laid upon the face of the King who was severely chastised.
Hideous deed! The face of the Creator spat upon. When his cross was placed between the two crosses of the condemned ones he was raised (alas!) upon the cross; it was very painful.

A crown of thorns was placed (this was severe excess) about his beautiful head; nails were driven through his feet, others through his hands.

~ *A World made Whole* ~

Be Thy right hand, O God, under my head,
Be Thy light, O Spirit, over me shining.
And the cross of the nine angels over me, down
From the crown of my head to the soles of my feet,
From the crown of my head to the soles of my feet.

O Jesu without offence, crucified cruelly,
Under ban of the wicked thou wert scourged,
The many evils done of me in the body!
That I cannot this night enumerate,
That I cannot this night enumerate.

O Thou Ring of the blood of truth,
Cast me not from Thy covenant,
Exact not from me for my transgressions,
Nor omit me in Thy numbering,
Nor omit me in Thy numbering.

~ Carmina Gadelica ~

GOD
THE CREATOR

1   Recap   (5 mins)

Share in twos your experience of using the Caim and any thoughts on reconciliation, victory of the Cross and outreach you may have had.

2   The Celtic View of God   (25 mins)

Celtic Christianity reflected the life-style of the Celts. It was an every-day religion; it permeated throughout all they did. It was joyous, full of praise and adoration, of music and of dancing. Their earthly king was one of them, often living within their village area, facing the same problems and easily approachable. Their heavenly king was regarded in the same way. So it was normal to discuss their problems with God, and expect him to share in the joy of the freshly baked bread, or the cream of the milk, the worries of calving, or to be given the care of the sheep left on the hillside – after all he was the great shepherd so a few sheep would be easy for him!

So God is here with us. He is concerned for all our sorrows and joys – however small. He is part of our lives at all times, easily approachable. He is not around only on Sundays, nor is he so far above us that we can barely approach him. There is a Celtic saying which emphasises that we do not need to search for God or go on pilgrimages to find him – for God is always with us.

> *God is here, now:*
> *To go to Rome*
> *is much trouble, little profit.*
> *The King whom you seek there*
> *Unless you bring Him with you, you will not find.*

Individually

- Read the first part of the Resource Sheet for this Session on pages 46-47.

Move into small groups of four or five. Ask each group to concentrate on one question (a different one for each group) and only go on to the others if they have time. Then invite the groups to share together a little of their discussion on their main question.

Discuss
(in groups of four or five)

- Suggest some circumstances in which we are particularly aware of God being close to us. Can you say why we are more aware of God at these times?
- Consider a situation when we feel God is distant. What effect might it have to become aware of his closeness. How can we do this?
- Celtic Christians believe that God was concerned about every detail of their lives. Nowadays, some Christians say that they should not bother God with trivial things. Do you think you should pray about little things or only really important matters?

3   God the Creator

(a)   *God made the World*
      and he was pleased with it   (15 mins)

Individually

Read the prayers in the second section of the Resource
Sheet for this Session on pages 48-51;
... then **read aloud** Genesis 1: 20-25.

The Celts found God in nature, regarding it as the 'Primary Scriptures'
from which they could learn directly about him. Many Celts found
their own space – places where they could be alone – where they lived
permanently or retreated to regularly. Some of these were in woods, but
many were on small islands or promontories where the gales and the
sea were very near. These Celtic hermits would go out into the gales
and feel God near to them. The Celts recognised all of nature as being
created by God and therefore revealing something of God. By contact
with nature they could draw close to God. (This is called *panentheism*).
This is quite different to the pagan idea that all things can be worshipped as gods (*ie pantheism*). The two words are similar, but the ideas
are very different!

Individually

Be still for a few moments and think of a wood, stream,
mountain, sea view, or any place where you have felt God
close to you at some time in the past, or where you think
you may find him. Spend the time thinking about God
revealed in nature and what it can teach us.

Nature is God's Creation and the Celts believed that all created things
joined in worshipping the Creator. So Christians would walk in the

woodlands and see them as temples to God. They would admire the beauty of flowers and listen for the bird song, singing of the glory of God. One Hebridean lady told of her mother chiding her as a girl, saying: 'Listen to the birds praising God – should we then be silent?'

Some of today's hymns echo this Celtic view of nature. The Celts loved music and laughter and most of their prayers were actually sung. Their religion was joyous. We have lost the music they used, but it would have been popular folk music. Often a travelling poet/singer would arrive in a village, the villagers would gather round in the evening and he would lead them in songs, well-known and new. Let the group imagine this is a similar Celtic evening.

Play or recite

- Join together playing and singing 'All God's Creatures have a Place in the Choir' (pages 115-116); *or*
- Recite the song with a leader saying the verses and the group joining together in the chorus.

Listen for the Celtic ideas in the song.

All God's Creatures got a Place in the Choir

Chorus   All God's creatures got a place in the choir.
Some sing low and some sing higher,
Some sing out loud on the telephone wire,
Some just clap their hands or paws
    or anything they've got. Now –

Verse 1 Listen to the beast that's the one on the bottom
Where the bull frog croaks
Hippopotamus moans and groans with a great to do
The old brown cow goes moo.
Chorus ...

Verse 2 Dogs and cats they take out the middle
Where the honey bee hums, cricket fiddles,
Donkey brays and the pole cat shrieks,
Old grey badger sighs.
Chorus ...

Verse 3 Listen to the top with the little birds singing,
On the melodies the high notes ringing,
the hoot owl screams at everything,
blackbird disagrees.
Chorus ...   *~ Modern Folk Song ~*

(b)   *God is creating now*   (15 mins)

The Celts felt God did not stop creating once the world was made, but
that he was at work creating at all times. So they would pray for sun and
rain, for fertility of crops and animals, and give thanks for all these
things. They saw the world as God's workshop. Imagine for a moment
that you are in an art gallery looking at a famous painting, or at a copy
of it at home. Now imagine you have had the privilege of watching the
artist create that picture – or have been in a pottery watching a potter
throw a vase, or a sculptor create a statue. How much more we would
treasure that work of art because we had watched the artist creating it.
This is how the Celts saw our world. We can watch God at work in it.
People may scoff at religion, saying 'Show us your God'. We may not be
able to show them God himself, but we can show God at work. We can

stop, be still, and watch God here and now. We can exist in the present and share time with our God who is alive and at work in our midst.

The world is God's gift to us that he is working on at this minute. We can watch God at work now. We can pray and contemplate in the present, not merely what God has created, but praise him for what he is doing now.

Reflection

- Look at the picture, plant or flower arrangement provided for this Session. Reflect on God creating it. Think about what God might be saying through it.
- Play a tape of some quiet music. End the reflection by playing a tape of 'O Lord my God, when I in awesome wonder' (*Songs of God's People* no. 86), or hand out the words for the group to read together, or silently.

(c) Man's Relationship to God   (5 mins)

God made the world and was pleased with it. He made man and the Celts believed God was also pleased with man. They felt beauty and love were there for God to share with man and for man to express his love of God and his neighbour. This was in contrast to the teaching of Augustine, and later the Puritans, who saw beauty as a distraction from God and a temptation to sin.

(d) Man's Relationship to the World   (15 mins)

The Celts felt that the world is a gift to us to cherish. It has not been given to us to use however we choose. It has been said that if, at the

Synod of Whitby, we had accepted the Celtic Church, we shouldn't now have an ecology problem. Although Celtic spirituality continued to influence British Christianity for some time, Augustinian Christianity gradually gained supremacy over much of Britain. Celtic Christians could not have exploited nature in the way recent generations of Western Christians have done and created the problems we now face.

Discuss (in groups of four or five)
Taking care of God's World

It has been suggested that each family could help care for our planet by changing our own lifestyles: eg by buying more environmentally-friendly products, even if more expensive; by conserving water by installing toilets which use less water; by having water meters fitted; or by walking and cycling more often.
- Can you suggest other measures we could take?
- To what extent do you feel it is part of our Christian response to God's world to take such measures?
- What other environmental issues particularly concern you? What action do you feel God is asking Christians to take?

---

4 Group Prayer   (10 mins)

Pray, using prayers from the sheet (pp 46-51) – open prayer or silently. Think particularly about God's presence with us at all times and praise him both for the creation he has done and for the work he is doing now. Pray too about the environment and how we should respond, on an individual and a national level, to the problems we face. You might like to open or close with a Caim prayer.

RESOURCE SHEET 2

GOD THE CREATOR

THE CLOSENESS OF GOD

The Heavenly Banquet

I would like to have the men of Heaven
In my own house:
With vats of good cheer
Laid out for them.

I would like to have them be cheerful
In their drinking,
I would like to have Jesus too
Here amongst them.

I would like a great lake of beer
For the King of Kings,
I would like to be watching Heaven's family
Drinking it through all eternity.

~ A World made Whole ~

I on Thy Path

God over me, God under me,
God before me, God behind me,
I on Thy path O God
Thou O God, in my steps.

~ Carmina Gadelica ~

Night prayer

I lie in my bed
as I would lie in the grave,
Thine arm beneath my neck
Thou Son of Mary victorious.

~ Carmina Gadelica ~

God's clasp

May the everlasting Father Himself take you
In His own generous clasp,
In His own generous arm.

~ Carmina Gadelica ~

Before me

Be Thou a smooth way before me,
Be Thou a guiding star above me,
Be Thou a keen eye behind me,
This day, this night, for ever.

I am weary and forlorn,
Lead Thou me to the land of angels;
Methinks it were time I went for a space
To the court of Christ, to the peace of heaven.

~ Carmina Gadelica ~

THE CREATOR AND CREATION

The Primary Scriptures

'If you want to know the creator, understand created things.'

~ *St Columbanus* ~

To the New Moon

He who created thee
    created me likewise;
He who gave thee weight and light
    Gave to me life and death.

~ *Carmina Gadelica* ~

Where is God's dwelling?

He has his dwelling around heaven and earth and sea and all that in them is. He inspires all, he quickens all, he dominates all, he supports all. He lights the light of the sun. He furnishes the light of the night. He has made springs in the dry land. He has set stars to minister to the greater lights.

He is the God of heaven and earth, of sea and rivers, of sun and moon and stars, of the lofty mountains and the lowly valley, the God above heaven and under heaven.

~ A legendary response of St Patrick (*Threshold of Light*) ~

The voice of thunder

O God of the elemental might,
O God of the mysterious height,
O God of the stars and cloudsprings bright,
    Till the end of ends below,
     O King of kings to bestow!
     O King of kings to bestow!

Thy joy the joy of the raindrops' play.
Thy light the light of the lightning's spray
Thy war the war of the heavenly fray,
    Thy peace the peace of the bow,
    Thy peace the peace of the bow.

Thy pain the pain of groaning and clash,
Thy love the love of the sudden flash,
That lasts for aye like the music's crash,
    Till the end of ends below,
    Till the ends of ends below.

Thou pourest thy grace, refreshing shower,
Upon men in grief and duress hour,
Upon men in straits and danger's power,
    Without cease or stint to show,
    Without cease or stint to show.

~ Praying with Highland Christians ~

Almighty Creator

Almighty Creator, who hast made all things,
The world cannot express all thy glories,
Even though the grass and the trees should sing.

The Father has wrought so great a multitude of wonders
That they cannot be equalled.
No letters can contain them, no letters can express them.

He who made the wonder of the world
Will save us, has saved us.
It is not too great toil to praise the Trinity.

~ A World made Whole ~

Morning prayer

I believe, O God of all gods,
That Thou art the eternal Father of life:
I believe, O God of all gods,
That Thou art the eternal Father of love.

I believe, O Lord and God of the peoples,
That Thou art the creator of the high heavens,
That Thou art the creator of the skies above,
That Thou art the creator of the oceans below.

I believe, O Lord and God of the peoples,
That Thou art He who created my soul and set its warp.
Who created my body from dust and from ashes,
Who gave to my body breath and to my soul its possession.

~ Carmina Gadelica ~

Do a miracle for me

O Son of God, do a miracle for me, and change my heart; Thy having taken flesh to redeem me was more difficult than to transform my wickedness.

It is Thou who, to help me, didst go to be scourged by the Jews; Thou, dear child of Mary, art the refined molten metal of our forge.

It is Thou who makest the sun bright, together with the ice; it is Thou who createst the rivers and the salmon all along the river.

That the nut-tree should be flowering, O Christ, it is a rare craft; through Thy skill too comes the kernel, Thou fair ear of our wheat.

Though the children of Eve ill deserve the bird-flocks and the salmon, it was the immortal One on the cross who made both salmon and birds.

It is He who makes the flower of the sloe grow through the surface of the blackthorn, and the nut-flower on other trees: beside this what miracle is greater?

~ Threshold of Light ~

NEVER TOO BUSY
TO PRAY

1   Recap   (5 mins)

Share any experiences since the group last met of a greater awareness of God at work now, of his closeness, of our responsibility to our environment, or anything else relevant to the last two Sessions.

2   Never too busy to pray   (20 mins)

The Celtic prayers we still have are mainly the everyday prayers of the ordinary people. These were passed on from parents to children and were said, reverently but ritually, throughout the day. Some were for use individually, but many were for group use. These were either led by one person – for example, the mother who would say the *smooring* and *kindling* prayers; or they were said together – *eg* the weaving prayers. (A Celtic home fire was rarely put out. Each night it was covered to let it slowly smoulder – *smooring* – and each morning it would be revived – *kindling*.)

Celtic Prayers

Individually

- Take 5 minutes to read silently the Resource Sheet of Prayers on pages 66-73. The 'Blessing of the Car' on page 73 is a modern Celtic-style prayer.

Discuss
(in groups of four or five)

- Share your favourite prayer and the reason for your choice.
- Discuss the following possible reactions to the prayers:

1 Prayers said by rote have little real value;
2 Prayer is a private, personal thing. I would never pray out loud in a group;
3 If I was to bless the gas man when he came to sort out a problem, he would think I was mad!
4 If I prayed in public as I went about my daily life, it would be like flaunting my faith – showing off – and this would put people off;
5 I cannot pray for colds and things – they are too trivial to bother God with.

Share the main points of the discussion with the whole group.

3   Writing Celtic Prayers   (15 mins)

Many of us still say grace before meals, or say 'God bless' as people go to bed, or 'good bye' – a shortening of the prayer 'God be with you' – as people leave. Celtic praying had a number of advantages:

- The Celtic custom of praying aloud throughout the day meant faith was a shared, spoken thing. Everyone was aware of it and joined in, from the smallest child to the stranger. There was no need to decide how to share their faith – they were sharing it all the time:

- They prayed throughout the day so a day never passed without prayer;
- Nothing was too trivial for prayer;
- Celtic prayers allowed the tasks to speak of God and spiritual things.

Many of the prayers reminded the person of Scripture, while others used daily tasks and let God speak through them. Thus when kindling the fire, the person was led to pray for love for his neighbour; prayer for physical food led on to prayer for spiritual food, and so on. This is demonstrated by some of the prayers on the Resource Sheet.

Many of the Celtic prayers refer to tasks which are not relevant to the lives most of us lead – such as smooring the fire, milking the cow, and churning the butter.

Individually

- Write a Celtic prayer about one of your daily tasks – eg cleaning the house, driving the car, your work, *etc.* Use a Scriptural parallel or let the task evoke spiritual things.

4   Group Prayer   (15 mins)

Use this time of prayer …
- to share your own prayers;
- to share any prayers from the sheet that speak to you;
- to pray about everyday, maybe trivial, things.

5   A Celtic Dance   (15 mins)

Celts used dance in their worship. This dance is a farewell prayer-dance which you might like to use in the final Session (see p 108).

* Either let the group learn the tune and practice singing the words;
* *or* recite the words together until they become familiar (see p 117).

> May the road rise with you; (1)
> may the wind be always at your back. (2)
> May the sun shine warm upon your face; (3)
> may the rain fall soft upon your fields. (4)
> Until we meet again (5), may God hold you (6)
> in the hollow of His hand. (7)

The Dance – *Preparations*

* Let everyone stand in a circle making an even number of people (the leader should join in if needed to make the numbers even) – person 'A' ... 'B' ... 'A' ... 'B' – all the way round.
* Then, without the music, walk through the dance saying the words and doing the actions.

The Dance – *Directions*

(1) Hold hands and walk slowly round clockwise.
(2) Loosen hands and raise them above your head.
      Circle slowly clockwise on the spot.

(3) People 'A' turn to right, 'B's to left, so that you are facing a partner. Join hands with your partner by placing the hands palm against palm in front of your chest. Slowly move your palms up, out, down and back to make two circles.

(4) Part hands.
Raise them to eye level, palms facing your partner's, and let them slowly fall to imitate rain.

(5) Join hands, take one small step to the left, 'A's moving inwards and 'B's outwards.

(6) Take another larger step, this time to right so that 'A's are on outside of circle, 'B's on inside.

(7) Loose hands and walk on in direction you are facing to meet a new partner.

The Dance

When the group are reasonably comfortable with the dance movements, sing or recite the words and the dance. This is a progressive dance, so repeat the blessing four or five times, or until you are back with your original partner.

---

6   Celtic Art   (20 mins)

Celtic art was a highly sophisticated art form long before the Celts became Christians. Their art was usually abstract, consisting of flowing lines, spirals, key and weaving patterns. The spirals reminded the Celts of the whorls in the water, the movement in the outer rings gradually giving way to the still centre. This helped them to reflect on the busyness of our outer selves surrounding a still centre where we can meet with God. The flowing lines reminded them of the continuity of life. The key patterns are associated with the maze and religious dances which were originally pagan but adapted by the Celtic Christians. The weaving patterns were made of one continuous line symbolising our continuous spiritual growth.

Weaving patterns are found on many of the ancient crosses as well as in much of Celtic art. They are also to be seen on many modern war memorials. The weaving of cloth was an important part of domestic life. As the women created the cloth by weaving in the patterns, so they thought of God weaving in and out of their lives.

Individually

- Spend a few minutes looking at the pattern from the St Madoes Stone and the prayers on the following pages.

St Madoes Stone

The Weaver

I weave into my life this day
The Presence of God upon my way,
I weave into my life this hour
The mighty God and all his power.
I weave into my sore distress
His peace and calm and no less
I weave into my steps so lame
Healing and helping of His name.
I weave into the darkest night
Strands of God shining bright,
I weave into each deed done
Joy and hope of the Risen Son

~ Tides and Seasons ~

A Weaving Pattern

The weaving of peace be thine
Peace around thy soul entwine
Peace of the Father flowing free
Peace of the Son sitting over thee
Peace of the Spirit from thee and me
Peace of the One
Peace of the Three
A weaving of peace be upon thee.

Around thee twine the Three
The One the Trinity

The Father bind his love
The Son tie his salvation
The Spirit wrap his power
Make you a new creation
Around thee twine the Three
The encircling of the Trinity.

~ Edge of Glory ~

Weaving

I weave tonight
A Presence bright
I weave tonight
The sacred Light
Warp on woof.

I weave tonight
The Father's might
I weave tonight
The Saviour's fight
Warp on woof

I weave tonight
In Spirit's sight
I weave tonight
The Truine right
Warp on woof.

~ Tides and Seasons ~

The prayers ask God to weave himself into the person's life; they give thanks and recognition for where they see him at work. Some people interpret the patterns as the ups and downs of life. Another interpretation is that the pattern is our fate: the characteristics we are born with, the culture we grow up in. Only Jesus has the power to break the threads of our life and set us free. So some early stones have the cross cutting through the weaving pattern. This can speak to us of freeing us from prejudice, from all the injustices we take for granted – such as you and I should have cheap coffee for breakfast, whilst workers who cultivate the coffee are starving through low wages, and many other doubtful ideas we have inherited and rarely question.

Refer to the 'Reflection' on the following page.

Reflection

Use the weaving pattern from the St Madoes stone for a
time of reflection in any of the following ways:

1 Chose a specific time of your life – today, this week,
   a time of an important decision, or sadness – and
   reflect on the ups and downs during that period.
   Recall how Christ was with you at those times.

2 Think how Christ has woven himself into your life. In
   what ways did you invite him? In what ways was he
   just there? What can you learn from this and in what
   ways can you invite him to weave himself into all the
   parts of your life during the next few days?

3 Think of some of your inherited assumptions. Where
   is Christ trying to break through your inherited
   weaving of life? What is he trying to say to you?

When reflecting, it is often helpful to have something
trivial to do in order to keep our mind on the job. So
may I suggest you follow the weaving pattern with a
pencil, noticing when it goes under and when it goes
over and pausing to give God time to speak.

RESOURCE SHEET 3

NEVER TOO BUSY TO PRAY

PRAYING AS YOU WORK

For dressing ...

Thanks be to Thee, O God, that I have risen today,
    To the rising of this life itself;
May it be to Thine own glory, O God of every gift,
    And to the glory of my soul likewise.

O great God, aid Thou my soul
    With the great aiding of thine own mercy;
Even as I clothe my body with wool.
    Cover Thou my soul with the shadow of Thy wing.

Help me to avoid every sin,
    And the source of every sin to forsake,
And as the mist scatters on the crest of the hills,
    May each ill haze clear from my soul, O God.

~ Carmina Gadelica ~

Blessing of the Kindling

I will kindle my fire this morning
In the presence of the holy angels of heaven,

Without malice, without jealousy, without envy,
Without fear, without terror of anyone under the sun,
But the Holy Son of God to shield me.

God, kindle thou in my heart within
A flame of love to my neighbour,
To my foe, to my friend, to my kindred all,
To the brave, to the knave, to the thrall,
O Son of the loveliest Mary,
From the lowliest thing that liveth,
To the Name that is highest of all.

~ *Carmina Gadelica* ~

Prayer for Light ...

Lord grant me, I pray thee in the name of Jesus Christ the Son, my God, that love which knows no fall so that my lamp may feel the kindling touch and know no quenching, may burn for me and for others may give light.

Do thou, Christ, deign to kindle our lamps, our Saviour most sweet to us, that they may shine continually in thy temple, and receive perpetual light from thee the perpetual light, so that our darkness may be driven from us.

~ Prayer of St Columbanus (*Threshold of Light*) ~

For milking the cow ...

Come, Mary, and milk my cow,
Come, Bride and encompass her,
Come, Columba, the benign,
And twine thine arms around my cow.

~ Carmina Gadelica ~

For churning butter ...

Come thou, Bridget, handmaid calm,
Hasten the butter on the cream,
See thou impatient Peter yonder
Waiting the buttered bannock white and yellow.

Come thou Mary Mother mild,
Hasten the butter on the cream;
See thou Paul and John and Jesus
Waiting the gracious butter yonder.

~ Carmina Gadelica ~

Thanks after food ...

Thanks be to Thee, O God,
Praise be to Thee, O God,
Reverence be to Thee, O God,
For all Thou hast given me.

As thou didst given life corporeal
To earn me my worldly food,
So grant to me life eternal
To show forth Thy glory.

Grant me grace throughout my life,
Grant me life at the hour of my death;
Be with me, O God, in casting off my breath,
O God, be with me in the deep currents.

~ Carmina Gadelica ~

For healing ...

Put Thy salve to my sight,
Put Thy balm to my wounds,
Put Thy linen robe to my skin,
O Healing Hand,
O Son of the God of Salvation.

~ Carmina Gadelica ~

Journeying

God be shielding thee by each dropping sheer,
God make every pass an opening to appear,
God make to thee each road a highway clear,
And may he take thee in the clasp
Of his own two hands' grasp.

~ Carmina Gadelica ~

The Helmsman

God of the elements, glory to thee
For the lantern-guide of the ocean wide;
On my rudder's helm may thine own hand be,
And thy love abaft on the heaving sea.

~ Praying with Highland Christians ~

God of the Sea

O God of the heaving sea,
Give the wave fertility,
Weed for enriching the ground,
Our life-giving pouring sound.

~ Praying with Highland Christians ~

For protecting animals ...

May the herding of Columba
Encompass you going and returning.
Encompass you in strath and on ridge
And on the edge of each rough region.

~ Carmina Gadelica ~

For reaping ...

God, bless Thou Thyself my reaping,
Each ridge, and plain, and field,
Each sickle curved, shapely, hard,
Each ear and handful on the sheaf.

Bless each maiden and youth,
Each woman and tender youngling,
Safeguard them beneath Thy shield of strength,
And guard them in the house of saints,
Guard them in the house of saints.

~ Carmina Gadelica ~

For smooring the fire at night ...

The peat is divided into three, the first is laid down in the name of the God of Life, the second the God of peace, the third the God of Grace. The circle is then covered with ashes in the name of the Three of Light

The Sacred Three
To save
To shield
To surround
The hearth
The house
The household

This eve
This night
O! this eve
This night
Each single night
~ Carmina Gadelica ~

Bed Blessing

I am lying down tonight
With Mary mild and with her Son,
With the Mother of my King,
Who is shielding me from harm.

I will not lie down with evil,
Nor shall evil lie down with me,
But I will lie down with God,
And God will lie down with me.
~ Carmina Gadelica ~

Undressing Prayer

O God, lift from me mine anguish sore,
O God, lift from me what I abhor,
O God, lift from me vanity's store,
And lighten my soul in thy love's light.

As I shed off my clothing at night,
Grant that I shed off my conflict-plight,
as vapours lift off the hill-crests white,
Lift thou my soul from the mist of death.

~ Praying with Highland Christians ~

Blessing of the Car

Bless the key – turn me to you
Bless the wheel, may all my thoughts go to and from you
Bless the steering, may I always keep on your way
Bless the gears, may I move at the speed you want
Bless the mirror, may I keep looking at Jesus your image
and may I keep all others on my road in sight
Bless the brakes, may I stop well short of danger
Bless the windows, may I see and know it is all your world as I travel
Bless the lights, may I use your inspiration when it is dark
Bless the accelerator, may I be anxious to move fast towards you
Bless my whole car, may I travel with you in my heart, always, all places.

~ Sister Rita McLoughlin ~

THE
TRINITY

1   Recap   (5 mins)

Invite the group to share any experiences of using Celtic prayers and writing their own examples since the last Session. Share too how they felt about the Celtic Dance on page 58 and their participation in it. Invite any member of the group who has written a prayer, and who would like to share it, to do so.

2   The Trinity   (30 mins)

Individually

Read the prayers on Adoration on pages 84-85 of the Resource Sheet at the end of this Session.

Read aloud

2 Corinthians 13: 14 and 1 Peter 1: 2.

The Celts were very conscious of the three-fold nature of God. They did not develop a deep theology of the Trinity, but they emphasised the different aspects of Father, Son and Spirit in many of their prayers. Many of their daily tasks were done three times, and this fitted into the pattern of repetition associated with Trinitarian prayers such as the Washing Prayer on page 86.

Celtic prayers tended to focus on one theme and take time to allow the mind to work around this theme. So, for example, in the prayer for blessing on pages 85-86, all that is being asked is that God should cherish me, make me holy and keep me from stumbling, yet the way it is written allows us to pray this slowly and prayerfully. This type of prayer lends itself readily to adoration, something that many find hard to put into words nowadays.

Read aloud

One of the Adoration prayers on pages 84-85.

Reflection on the Trinity

Spend a few minutes thinking in silence about the Trinity. Consider to what extent you are aware of the threefold aspect of God. Most people emphasise one aspect of God more than the other two. Here are a few thoughts on our experience of God. [Leave a few moments between each thought for the group to reflect on it.]

- Those who emphasise God the *Father* may be very conscious of the awe, power, and majesty of God. They may also feel that God is distant, remote and uninvolved in their lives;
- Those who emphasise God the *Son* may be very conscious of Jesus as friend, companion and fellow-sufferer, but may feel that He is fairly powerless and lacking in divinity;
- Those who emphasise God the *Holy Spirit* may feel the gifts of the Spirit are extremely important; they may feel at home with the charismatic groups and very joyful worship. However, they may place less emphasis on the cross, the need for redemption, and the sacrificial life.

Writing Prayers to the Trinity

Individually

Read the prayers on pages 85-88.

Write a prayer to the Trinity, thinking of the different attributes of God the Father, Son and Holy Spirit.

Share briefly how this felt – in pairs, small groups or in one large group.

3   Symbols for the Holy Spirit   (15 mins)

The Wild Goose

What words do you associate with wild geese?
- *eg* free ... wild ... powerful

The Dove

What words do you associate with doves?
- *eg* pretty ... tame ... source of food ... pure ... clean

Spend a few minutes sharing these ideas about geese and doves.

For most Christians the traditional symbol for the Holy Spirit is the dove, but there is scant Biblical authority for this. There are only a few references in the Bible to the dove – for example, the dove which came

79

down at Jesus' baptism (Mark 1:11), or Noah sending out a dove from
the ark (Genesis 8:8), although this has nothing obvious to do with the
Holy Spirit.

At Pentecost the symbols of tongues of fire and a rushing wind are used.
These are more Scriptural since the Old Testament word for 'Spirit' was
Ruach, which could mean 'breath' but could also refer to a very strong
desert wind, a whirlwind, or tornado.

When God appeared to Moses it was as a burning bush (Exodus 3: 4).
Fire can be both a tame hearth fire and an inferno.

The Celtic symbol for the Holy Spirit was the wild goose. In many
ways it fits in better with the Biblical symbols of fire and wind, although
I have found no reference to it in the Bible.

Individual reflection

- Is your Holy Spirit a **dove** – under your control, to be
  used when you need it?
- Or is it a **goose** – wild, coming to you when it decides,
  controlling you?
- Who's in charge – the Holy Spirit or you?

---

4   Prayers of Protection   (15 mins)

The Celts were very conscious of the dangers of their world – with
justification! Are we aware of the dangers of our world?

- There are dangers which face us from other people: *eg* vandalism, riots, assault, robbery, loss of job, slander, global warming, war, famine;
- There are dangers we can be lured into: *eg* drugs, assumptions of the Western world;
- There are injustices which we take for granted and are often unaware of: *eg* business practices you have to accept to keep your job, buying inessential goods, wasting resources by a thoughtless lifestyle.

Discuss
(in groups of four or five)

What are the dangers we face today?

Consider:
- physical dangers such as accidents, illness, poverty;
- temptation such as recreational drugs, advertising, peer pressure;
- pressure to lead life following Jesus less closely than we would really like to.

In what ways is the situation worse for those in the Western (rich?) world?

5   Scripture Prayers   (15 mins)

The Celtic monks spent much of their time reading the Bible. They had a special love of St John's Gospel, the Magnificat and the Psalms.

Read aloud

John 1: 1-14.

Think what it would have meant to the Celts who saw God at work in all the natural world; who believed that God created all of us and all of nature, and that he loved it all.

They also used the Scriptures in their prayers. Read the prayers on the Resource Sheet ('Prayers from Scripture' on pages 89-91). The first ones remind us of things God has done in the past, and is therefore presumably capable of doing today. This strengthens our faith. Others remind us of stories about Jesus. In Celtic times only a few people could read. Scripture based prayers helped to give them a knowledge of the Scriptures – they *lived* with them.

Reflection

Make sure that every member of the group has access to a Bible.

Either reflect on <u>one</u> of these passages:

- John 1 : 1-14
- Luke 1 : 46-55, or 68-79
- Psalm 8, 65, 93, 96, 148

or try to write a prayer based on passages of Scripture.

6   Group Prayer   (10 mins)

Join together to share a time of prayer, concentrating on:

- Adoration of God;
- Praying to the Trinity;
- Prayers for our own protection.

Prayers written during this Session might be prayed aloud at this time.

FOR THE NEXT SESSION

The next Session, being the last Session, will end with a Celtic-style service. It is hoped that anyone who feels able to, will contribute something to this service. You could bring a prayer, a hymn (probably a modern one), a passage of Scripture, a poem, or something from nature which you feel is appropriate to a Celtic-style service. Let the group leader know what you wish to contribute so that the order of service can be worked out well in advance of the next Session. Remember that if you wish the whole group to join in, then you will need to have the words available.

RESOURCE SHEET 4

THE TRINITY

ADORATION

I bow before the Father who made me
I bow before the Son who saved me
I bow before the Spirit who guides me
In love and adoration
    I give my lips
    I give my heart
    I give my mind
    I give my strength
I bow and adore Thee
Sacred Three, The Ever One,
The Trinity.

~ Edge of Glory ~

I am bending my knee
In the eye of the Father who created me,
In the eye of the Son who died for me,
In the eye of the Spirit who cleansed me,
    In love and desire.

~ Carmina Gadelica ~

The Father who created me
    With eye benign beholdeth me.
The Son who dearly purchased me
    With eye divine enfoldeth me,
The Spirit who so altered me
    With eye refining holdeth me.

In friendliness and love the Three
Behold me when I bend the knee.
                        ~ God in Our Midst ~

GENERAL PRAYERS TO THE TRINITY

In the name of the Father,
In the name of the Son,
In the name of the Spirit,
    Three in One;

Father cherish me,
Son cherish me,
Spirit cherish me,
    Three all-kindly.

God make me holy,
Christ make me holy,
Spirit make me holy,
    Three all-holy.

Three aid my hope,
Three aid my love,

Three aid my eye,
    And my knee from stumbling,
    My knee from stumbling.
        ~ *Carmina Gadelica* ~

I lay me down with Thee, O Jesus
and mayest Thou be about my bed,
The oil of Christ be upon my soul,
The Apostle's Creed be above my head.
O Father who wrought me
O Son who bought me
O Spirit who sought me
Let me be Thine.
        ~ *Religious Songs* ~

[Said when washing ...]

The three palmfuls
Of the sacred Three
To preserve thee
From every envy
Evil eye and death;
The palmful of the God of Life,
The palmful of the Christ of Love,
The palmful of the Spirit of Peace,
Triune of Grace.
        ~ *Carmina Gadelica* ~

Spirit give me of Thine abundance,
Father, give me of Thine wisdom,
Son, give me in my need,
Jesus beneath the shelter of Thy shield.

I lie down tonight,
With the Triune of my strength,
With the Father, with Jesus,
With the Spirit of might.

~ Carmina Gadelica ~

Be the eye of God dwelling with you,
The foot of Christ in guidance with you,
The shower of the Spirit pouring on you,
Richly and generously.

~ Carmina Gadelica ~

Five Prayers for protection ...

The keeping of God upon thee in every pass,
The shielding of Christ upon thee in every path,
The bathing of the Spirit upon thee in every stream
In every land and sea thou goest.

~ Carmina Gadelica ~

Be the great God between thy two shoulders
To protect thee in thy going and in thy coming.
Be the Son of Mary Virgin near thy heart,
And be the perfect Spirit upon thee pouring –
Oh, the perfect Spirit upon thee pouring!

~ Carmina Gadelica ~

Father us surround
Every foe confound

Jesus entwine
Keep us thine

Spirit enfold
In thy hold

Sacred three enthral
To thee we call.

~ Edge of Glory ~

God with me protecting,
The Lord with me directing,
The Spirit with me strengthening
For ever and for evermore,
For ever and evermore, Amen.
Chief of chiefs, Amen.

~ Carmina Gadelica ~

May God shield us by each sheer drop,
May Christ keep us on each rock-path,
May the Spirit fill us on each bare slope,
as we cross hill and plain,
Who live and reign
One God for ever. Amen.

~ God in Our Midst ~

PRAYERS FROM SCRIPTURE

God the Father all-powerful, benign,
Jesu the Son of tears and of sorrow,
With thy co-assistance, O Holy Spirit!

The Three-One, ever-living, ever-mighty, everlasting,
Who brought the Children of Israel through the Red Sea,
And Jonah to land from the belly of the great creature of the ocean.

Who brought Paul and his companions in the ship,
From the torment of the sea, from the dolour of the waves,
From the gale that was great, from the storm that was heavy.

Sain and shield and sanctify us,   sain = heal
Be Thou, King of the elements, seated at our helm,
And lead us in peace to the end of our journey.

~ Carmina Gadelica ~

Thou who guided Noah over the flood waves, hear us
Who with thy word recalled Jonah from the abyss, deliver us
Who stretched forth thy hand to Peter as he sank, help us O Christ
Son of God, thou didst marvellous things of the Lord with our Fathers,
Be favourable in our day also,
Stretch forth thy hand from on high.

~ The Stowe Missal ~

Save me, O Jesus whom Thy mother's kin rejected,
   as Thou didst save Jacob from his brother's hands.
Save me from cause of every disease
   as Thou didst save Job from the devil's tribulations
Save me as Thou didst save Patrick from the poison at Tara,
Save me as Thou didst Kevin from the falling mountain.

~ Onegus ~

The Children of Israel, God taking them,
Through the Red Sea, obtained a path,
They obtained the quenching of their thirst
From a rock that might not by craftsmen be hewn.

To whom does tremble the voice of the wind?
To whom become tranquil strait and ocean?
To Jesus Christ, Chief of each saint.

~ Carmina Gadelica ~

For use at a meeting ...

O Jesus, son of God, who was silent before Pilate, do not allow us to loose our tongues without thinking on what we have to say and how we may say it.

On the sea ...

In the name of God who made a pathway of the waves may he bring us safely home at the end of the day.

> Thou Being who Jonah didst safely land
> Out of the bag of the sow of the sea.
> Bring thou myself to the beckoning strand
> With lading and ship entrusted to me.

On starting a journey ...

> I will follow you, O Lord, wherever you go,
> for you have the words of eternal life.

Home brewing ...

May he who made wine of water at the marriage feast of Cana put strength and vigour into this water.

Grace before meals ...

May the blessing of the five loaves and the two fishes which God shared among the five thousand be ours. May the King who did the sharing bless our sharing and co-sharing.

~ from An Introduction to Celtic Christianity ~

'ST PATRICK'S
BREASTPLATE'

1   Preparation for Service   (5 mins)

As this is the final Session, we will be closing with a short Celtic-style service (see page 108). At the end of Session 4 the group were asked to contribute an item to the service – a picture or floral decoration, a poem, hymn, prayer or Bible reading. Group members should have indicated briefly by now what they would like to contribute, so that the leader can decide on the order for the service.

2   Introduction to 'St Patrick's Breastplate'   (5 mins)

This prayer is one of the best known Celtic prayers. The earliest written version probably dates from the eighth century. It is certainly in the tradition of Patrick and may well have been handed down orally from the saint. This prayer can be seen to incorporate many of the aspects of Celtic Christianity which we have been exploring. However it is first and foremost a prayer of protection and to understand it we need to appreciate our own need for protection.

Prayer of claiming protection

This is not a prayer of *petition for* protection. It is a prayer of *claiming* the power of God to protect. It is similar to the Caim prayers: not a magic way of encircling yourself, so much as a recognition of what is there already.

Last Session we looked at the need for protection in the Celtic world, and also in our own lives today. Unless we are very conscious of our own vulnerability and our own need for divine protection, this prayer will mean little.

Individual Reflection

Spend a couple of minutes in silence thinking again of the many things we need protection from: eg terrorism, drunk drivers, the temptations of capitalism, the dominance of secular attitudes, our own feelings of inability to do anything about it – and recognise our need for God's protection.

We are now rediscovering that God's power – as seen in Creation, in the life of Jesus and in the early Church – is not a thing of history, but something available to us now if only we will claim it. However, the traditional Churches have often been frightened by this and those who claim to experience God's power today are sometimes considered slightly eccentric. Nevertheless we continue to hear about healing miracles from many sources and people do talk about experiencing God's power in their lives today. This power is always available – and available to everyone – if only we believe and claim it.

This is the message of this prayer:

> *Look at the power of God*
> *as we have seen it in the life of Jesus*
> *and in Creation.*
> *This power is available to us today*
> *Claim it!*

The Trinity

The prayer at the bottom of page 96 starts and finishes with a call to the holy power of the Trinity.

- It reminds us of the power of God seen in Creation;
- It reminds us of the power shown in the life of Christ;
- It acknowledges that these powers are available to us today, which is the work of the Spirit.

God the Creator

The prayer resonates with the belief that the power of God is revealed in Creation and that this power is available to protect us.

Many people are familiar with the version of 'St Patrick's Breastplate' written by Mrs Alexander as the hymn, 'I bind unto myself today'. The version on pages 111-114 is from an eighth century manuscript, recently translated by N D O'Donoghue, and the following Reflection owes much to his chapter in James Mackey's book *An Introduction to Celtic Christianity*.

3   Reflection on verses I-IV   (20 mins)

Verse I begins by calling on the whole power of the Trinity.

The first verse echoes the message from Paul to the Romans that 'If God is for us, who can be against us?'

Read aloud

- Verses I-IV of 'St Patrick's Breastplate' (pp 111-112).

Prayers like these were called 'Dressing Prayers' because they pulled on the power of God to surround and protect you in the same way as you pulled on a coat. They were often said at the start of the day. They reminded people to begin the day not in their own strength, but in the power of God.

Verse II reminds us of the power of God demonstrated in the life of Christ.

God is deeply involved in his world. This is supremely expressed in the incarnation. Although Christ was fully man, he was also God and the power of God is seen time and again in his life. This power of God which was seen in the life of Jesus is available to us today.

Verse III reminds us of the power of God demonstrated in the Heavenly Host – the Saints and Angels.

Christians who have lived, died and been recognised as having lead exemplary Christian lives can be used as heroes and role models. In today's world, however, many people see television, film, music or sport as a source for heroes/heroines – like soap stars or footballers. Often these modern-day role models can be unreal cult figures, even violent and aggressive. People subconsciously mould themselves like their heroes.

Verse III encourages us to identify with prophets, Apostles, and all great Christians who have gone before us. It might be helpful to become familiar with the lives and prayers of some of these great Christians.

Celtic people were very conscious of the spirit world long before they became Christians. They felt the spirits lived alongside us, even though they were usually invisible to our eyes. These spirits were eternal and therefore gave hope of eternal life to men and women. Celtic Christians adapted this to a natural acceptance of the hierarchies of angels who were only just out of sight and could be called upon for aid.

Verse IV reminds us of the power of God demonstrated in Creation.

- 'The Earth is the Lord's and everything in it.'   (Psalm 24: 1)
- 'The place where you are standing is holy ground.'   (Exodus 3: 5)
- 'The Lord is in this place and I was not aware of it.' (Genesis 28: 16)

This is the prayer of a people who recognise God is still at work in his creation, and that creation reveals the creator. The power is creative and intimate, not a massive overshadowing, despite the fact that it is the heavenly God displayed in the marvellous creation of earth.

This is God's world which we hold in trust.

- We are reminded of our ecological responsibilities which we considered in Session 2;
- We are reminded that we can see God revealed in nature. The Celts loved to go out into the storms to feel the power of God;

- We are reminded that we should be at home in God's world, and that our faith should be grounded in worldly matters as well as in the spiritual relationship we have with God.

Take some natural object or a small picture of nature. Hold it and meditate on God's Creation, maybe using this verse from William Blake's 'Auguries of Innocence':

> *To see a World in a Grain of Sand,*
> *And heaven in a Wild Flower,*
> *Hold Infinity in the palm of your hand,*
> *And eternity in an hour.*

Discuss
(in groups of four or five)

The Power of God

- Which incident in the life of Jesus most greatly displays God's power for you? Why do you choose this particular incident? (Think of verse II of 'St Patrick's Breastplate' – Christ's birth, baptism, death, resurrection, or anything else during his life.)
- When you consider Creation, what for you most display's God's power? Why does it? (Think of verse III – the sun, moon, fire, lightning, wind, *etc.*)
- Can you recall any incident when you have been aware of the power of God helping you? (Think of verse III – the powers of the heavenly beings; and verse V – God's strength, wisdom, words to speak, insight when listening, *etc.*)

4   Reflection on Verses V-VIIa   (10 mins)

Read aloud

- Verses V-VIIa of 'St Patrick's Breastplate' on pages 112-113.

Verse V reminds us of the power of God himself.

Spend a few moments silently thinking of times in the immediate future when you will need to be directed, sustained, guided, given a vision.

Pray aloud

Pray aloud the following lines, leaving a few minutes silence after each line for group members to fill in particular incidents for which they wish this gift ...

I call on God's strength to direct me ....

I call on God's power to sustain me ....

I call on God's wisdom to guide me ....

I call on God's vision to light me ....

*Verses Vb-VII focuses on the many aspects of life
where we need God's power of protection.*

The Devil is described in the Bible as 'a liar and father of lies' (John 8: 44), capable of taking on the appearance of 'an angel of light' (2 Corinthians 11: 14). So protection is sought, not so much against the power of the demon, as of his snares. The Celts felt that this is a good world, where nature and people are all good, but in which there is evil at work, often disguised.

We acknowledge and call on the power of God for good. We need to recognise that there is also a power for evil which can equally well be exercised. The druids were still a force to be reckoned with at this time, but although most people of today do not believe in spells or in dark powers – such as spells cast by blacksmiths and lying heretics, as mentioned in section VI of the 'Breastplate' – there is still much evil around, if in a different form.

Discuss
(briefly in a large group)

Present-day Evils

- debt encouraged by unscrupulous door-to-door selling;
- youngsters introduced to drugs by pushers;
- the 'Third World debt';
- Acid Rain and damage caused to the Earth by CFCs;
- Easy availability of 'video nasties';
- Radiation leaks.

What other evils would you add to this list?

The evils of our life may be different, but they are all around us, without and within, and we still need protection against them.

These verses end with a prayer for protection against the evil chances of life – *eg* death by fire, poison, wounding, drowning, and so on.

5   Meditation on Verse 7b   (10 mins)

The Living Presence of Christ

Paul wrote to the Galatians:
> 'I no longer live but Christ lives in me.'   (Galatians 2: 20)

Let one person real aloud the following meditation, leaving short pauses between each section.

Christ beside, behind, beneath, above …

We are surrounded by Christ. These words make their own space around us and remind us of the Caim we can draw and fill with Christ's presence. However there is nothing 'private' about it. Christ around us gives a connectedness and a deep holy respect for all human relationships.

Christ within me …

This experience of total immersion in Christ gives joy and peace which percolates into the quiet depths of the spirit and never leaves us.

Christ before me ...

Whatever lies ahead you have been there before:

> *If I went up to heaven, you would be there;*
> *if I lay down in the world of the dead, you would be there.*
> *If I flew away beyond the east,*
> *or lived in the farthest place in the west,*
> *you would be there to lead me,*
> *you would be there to help me.*   *~ Psalm 139: 8-10 ~*

Christ behind me ...

Whatever has happened in the past you can forgive and heal.

Christ on my right ...

in all people who will enrich me.

Christ on my left ...

protecting me from all that may harm or hinder me.

Christ when I lie down ...

to sleep and be refreshed.

Christ when I sit down ...

when I stop and relax.

Christ when I arise ...

in the power of the Spirit to the new day and new opportunities.

Christ in the heart of every one who thinks of me ...

Even those who as yet do not know or love you.

Christ in the mouth of every one who speaks to me ...

Lord, help me to listen to other people and be truly present to them. Help me too to listen for your voice in the words of others.

Christ in the eye of every one that sees me ...

Let me see you, Lord, in others, and may they see you in me.

Christ in every ear that hears me

Lord, you are there with the listener. Help me to respect you and to respect the listener. Help me to reveal you in the words that I speak.

6   Conclusion to 'St Patrick's Breastplate'

We are back where we started – we have prayed through an unending circle. Let us become aware each day of a new knowledge of God the creator, the protector, the ever-present companion of today and every day through into eternity.

The 'Breastplate' ends by looking straight into the face of Christ:

> *To the Lord belongs salvation …*
> *May your salvation, Lord,*
> *be with us always.*

7   Reflective Discussion on the Series   (15 mins)

Discuss
(in small groups of four to five)

- Share two things which you feel have been important for you during this series.

- Share something from this series which you feel you would like to continue to use in your Christian life, or something which you would like to explore more deeply in the future.

8   'Open hand' Meditation   (5 mins)

We have spent a lot of time looking at and learning from the ideas of
our Celtic forebears. However, in simply putting forward their ideas
in words we have lost some of the half statements that lead us on to
our own questions and ideas which were an essential part of the poetic
nature of the Celts. So, to end this series we are going to spend a few
minutes with a meditation I feel the Celts would have appreciated.

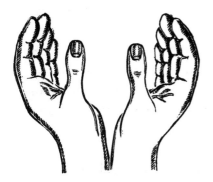

These Hands

These hands – God's hands
stretching out in blessing, in giving.

These hands – my hands
held out to receive all that my God
has to give to me.

These hands – my hands
offering up to God all that I am, the good, the bad,
the promises I make and try to keep.

These hands – God's hands
open to receive from me all that I know of myself to give to him.

These hands – whose hands? Giving or receiving?
They are our hands, Lord's, yours and mine,
joined together in the mutuality of giving and receiving.
This is the love of God.

Individually

Spend the next few minutes in silence looking at these hands and considering the inter-connectedness of giver and receiver and the continual circle formed by their relationship.

9   Short Celtic-style Service   (20 mins)

This should be allowed to happen almost spontaneously. The leader should try to be aware of all the contributions the group wish to make and then invite each person to offer their contribution at an appropriate point. The Circle Dance from Session 3 (see page 58) makes a very suitable ending to the service.

[The following outline is a guide only and you should feel free to develop the service as you wish.]

A Possible Outline for a Service

Opening prayer
with response:

Father in heaven hear us   (Leader)
Jesus our Saviour guide us   (Group)
Spirit our Strengthener hear us

Father in heaven guide us   (Leader)
Jesus our Saviour guide us   (Group)
Spirit our Strengthener guide us

Father in heaven help us   (Leader)
Jesus our Saviour help us   (Group)
Spirit our Strengthener help us

Father in heaven we love you   (Leader)
Jesus our Saviour we love you   (Group)
Spirit our Strengthener we love you

Father in heaven we need you   (Leader)
Jesus our Saviour we need you   (Group)
Spirit our Strengthener we need you

Father in heaven come to us   (Leader)
Jesus our Saviour come to us   (Group)
Spirit our Strengthener come to us

Three in One, One in Three   (Leader)
Give us peace evermore.

~ Edge of Glory ~

Hymn: 'Father we adore thee … '

Prayer
  of Confession: 'Weakly I go from the load within … '   [see p 13]

Reading: Psalm 8

                             Share a few thoughts on some insight from this
                             series, or bring something from nature and share
                             God revealed in it.

Prayer: Take a selection of prayers from the Resource sheets.

A Caim Prayer: From Resource Sheet 1 on pages 30-32;
                             or one written by a member of the group.

Blessing: Circle Dance
                             'May the road rise with you … '

Leader: 'To the Lord truly belongs salvation.'

Response: 'May your salvation, Lord, be with us always.'

RESOURCE SHEET 5

ST PATRICK'S BREASTPLATE

~ *Translated by N D O'Donoghue* ~

I   For my shield this day I call:
        A mighty power: The Holy Trinity!
        Affirming threeness
        Confessing oneness,
        In the making of all through love.

II   For my shield this day I call:
        Christ's power in his coming
        and in his baptising,
        Christ's power in his dying
        on the cross, his arising
        from the tomb, his ascending:
        Christ's power in his coming
        for judgment and ending.

III   For my shield this day I call:
        strong power of the seraphim,
        with angels obeying,
        and archangels attending,
        in the glorious company
        of the holy and risen ones,
        in the prayers of the fathers,
        in the visions prophetic
        and commands apostolic,

in virginal innocence,
in the deeds of steadfast men.

IV   For my shield this day I call:
Heaven's might,
Sun's brightness,
Moon's whiteness,
Fire's glory,
Lightning's swiftness,
Wind's wildness,
Ocean's depth,
Earth's solidity,
Rock's immobility.

V   For my shield this day I call:
God's strength to direct me,
God's power to sustain me,
God's wisdom to guide me,
God's vision to light me,
God's ear to my hearing,
God's word to my speaking,
God's hand to uphold me,
God's pathway before me,
God's shield to protect me,
God's legion's to save me:
from snares of the demons,
from evil enticements,
from failings of nature,
from one man or many
that seek to destroy me,
anear or afar.

VI   Around me I gather
      these forces to save
      my soul and my body
      from dark powers that assail me:
      against false prophesyings,
      against pagan devisings,
      against heretical lying
      and false gods all around me.
      Against spells cast by women,
      by blacksmiths, by Druids,
      against knowledge unlawful
      that injures the body,
      that injures the spirit.

VII

(a)   Be Christ this day my strong protector
       against poison and burning,
       against drowning and wounding,
       through reward wide and plenty ...

(b)   Christ beside me, Christ before me,
       Christ behind me, Christ within me,
       Christ beneath me, Christ above me,
       Christ to right of me, Christ to left of me;
       Christ in my lying, my sitting, my rising:
       Christ in heart of all who know me,
       Christ on tongue of all who meet me,
       Christ in eye of all who see me,
       Christ in ear of all who hear me.

VII   For my shield this day I call:
        A mighty power:
        The Holy Trinity!
        Affirming threeness
        Confessing oneness,
        In the making of all through love.

        For to the Lord belongs salvation,
        and to the Lord belongs salvation,
        and to Christ belongs salvation.
        May your salvation, Lord,
        be with us always.

MUSIC SHEET 1
ALL GOD'S CREATURES GOT A PLACE ...

~ Arranged by A G King ~

All God's creatures got a place in the choir . Some sing low and

some sing high-er some sing out loud on a tel-e phone wire,

some just clap their hands or paws or an-y thing they've got. Now,

Lis-ten to the beast that's the one on the bot-tom where the bull frog croaks

hip- po- pot- a-mus moans and groans with a great to do the

old brown cow goes moo. Dogs and cats,

MUSIC SHEET 2
MAY THE ROAD RISE WITH YOU
~ Arranged by A G King ~

RESOURCES

Audio-Cassettes

- 'Reaching Out'
  from Lee Abbey – by Simeon Wood and John Gerighty (published by Eagle, 59 Woodbridge Road, Guildford Surrey) (1991);
- 'Enchantment'
  by Stephen Rhodes (30 Barns Lane, Rushall, Walsall, West Midlands WS4 1HE) (1993);
- 'Inspirations'
  by Stephen Rhodes (St Paul Multimedia Productions UK, Middle Green, Slough, SL3 6BS) (1995);
- 'Skylark'
  by Hilary Rushmer (Swallow Studios, Sandbach, Cheshire).

Books

- *The Celtic Way* by Ian Bradley (published by Darton, Longman & Todd, London) (1993);
- *The Whole Earth Shall Cry Glory* by Revd George MacLeod (published by Wild Goose Publications, Glasgow) (1985);
- *Exploring Celtic Spirituality* by Ray Simpson (published by Hodder & Stoughton) (1995);
- *God in Our Midst* by Martin Reith (published by Triangle, SPCK, London) (1975);
- *The Celtic Alternative* by Shirley Toulson (published by Rider) (1987).

Posters with beautiful scenes of Nature are available from most Christian bookshops and can be used as a background for contemplating God the Creator.

REFERENCES

Adam David: *Edge of Glory* (Triangle, SPCK, London, 1987).

Adam David: *Tides and Seasons* (Triangle, SPCK, London, 1991).

Blake, William: 'Auguries of Innocence'.

Carmichael, Alexander: *Carmina Gadelica* (Floris Books, Edinburgh, 1992).

de Waal, Esther: *A World made Whole* (Fount, London, 1991).

de Waal, Esther and A M Allchin: *Threshold of Light* (Darton, Longman & Todd, London, 1988).

Hyde, Douglas: *The Religious Songs of Connacht* (Irish University Press, 1972).

Mackey, James P: *An Introduction to Celtic Christianity* (T&T Clark, Edinburgh, 1989).

MacLean, Alistair: *Hebridean Altars* (Moray Press, 1937).

McLean, G R D: *Praying with Highland Christians* (Triangle, SPCK, London, 1988).

O' Donoghue, N D: 'St Patrick's Breastplate', in James P Mackey: *An Introduction to Celtic Christianity* (T&T Clark, Edinburgh, 1989).

Reith, Martin: *God in Our Midst* (Triangle, SPCK, London, 1975).

ACKNOWLEDGEMENTS

*The Author and Publisher would like to acknowledge the following sources
for extracts quoted in this book:*

Extracts on pages 14, 31, 62-63, 84, 88, 109 from *Edge of Glory*
by David Adam, published 1987 by Triangle, SPCK, London.

Extracts on pages 12, 62, 63 from *Tides and Seasons*
by David Adam, published 1991 by Triangle, SPCK, London.

Extracts on pages 33-34, 48, 51, 67 from *Threshold of Light*
by A M Allchin and Esther de Waal, published and copyright 1986
by Darton, Longman & Todd Ltd and used by permission of the Publishers.

Extracts on pages 11, 34, 46, 50 from *A World made Whole* by Esther de Waal,
published 1991 by Fount, London.

Extracts on pages 13, 33, 86 from *The Religious Songs of Connacht*
by Douglas Hyde, published 1972 by Irish University Press.

Extracts on pages 90-91 and the translation of 'St Patrick's Breastplate'
by N D O'Donoghue on pages 111-114 from *An Introduction to Celtic Christianity*
by James P Mackey, published 1989 by T & T Clark Ltd
and used by permission of the Publishers.

Extracts on pages 12, 49, 70, 72-73 from *Praying with Highland Christians*
by G R D McLean, published 1988 by Triangle, SPCK, London.

Extracts on pages 15, 85, 88 from *God in Our Midst*
by Martin Reith, published 1975 by Triangle, SPCK, London.

'Blessing of the Car' by Sister Rita McLoughlin.

*While all reasonable efforts have been made to trace and acknowledge sources,
we apologise if any have been missed inadvertently. This will be amended at the next printing.*